PENPALS *for* Handwriting

Intervention Programme
Book 2 – Securing joins

Gill Budgell   Kate Ruttle

Supported by the
National Handwriting Association
Promoting good practice

Contents

Scope and sequence

Book 1 – Securing letter formation

1. Letter formation *i* and *l*
2. Letter formation *j*
3. Letter formation *t*
4. Letter formation *u* and *y*
5. Letter formation *r*
6. Letter formation *b*
7. Letter formation *n*
8. Letter formation *h*
9. Letter formation *m*
10. Letter formation *k*
11. Letter formation *p*
12. Letter formation *c*
13. Letter formation *a*
14. Letter formation *d*
15. Letter formation *o*
16. Letter formation *s*
17. Letter formation *g*
18. Letter formation *q*
19. Letter formation *e*
20. Letter formation *f*
21. Letter formation *v* and *w*
22. Letter formation *x* and *z*
23. Letter formation A, U, B, D
24. Letter formation C, G, E, F
25. Letter formation J, S, H, K
26. Letter formation I, L, T, M, N
27. Letter formation O, Q, P, R
28. Letter formation V, W, Y, X, Z
29. Numbers 1–10
31. Words and sentences with *i*
32. Words and sentences with *t*
33. Words and sentences with *u*
34. Words and sentences with *j*
35. Words and sentences with *r*
36. Words and sentences with *b*
37. Words and sentences with *n*
38. Words and sentences with *h*
39. Words and sentences with *m*
40. Words and sentences with *k*
41. Words and sentences with *p*
42. Words and sentences with *c*
43. Words and sentences with *a*
44. Words and sentences with *d*
45. Words and sentences with *o*
46. Words and sentences with *s*
47. Words and sentences with *g*
48. Words and sentences with *q*
49. Words and sentences with *e*
50. Words and sentences with *f*
51. Words and sentences with *v*, *w* and *x*
52. Words and sentences with *y* and *z*

Book 2 – Securing joins

1. Diagonal join to ascender from *a*
2. Diagonal join to ascender from *c*
3. Diagonal join to ascender from *e*
4. Diagonal join to ascender from *h* and *i*
5. Diagonal join to ascender from *k* and *l*
6. Diagonal join to ascender from *m* and *n*
7. Diagonal join to ascender from *t* and *u*
8. Diagonal join, no ascender, from *a*
9. Diagonal join, no ascender, from *c* and *d*
10. Diagonal join, no ascender, from *e*
11. Diagonal join, no ascender, from *h* and *i*
12. Diagonal join, no ascender, from *k* and *l*
13. Diagonal join, no ascender, from *m* and *n*
14. Diagonal join, no ascender, from *q*
15. Diagonal join, no ascender, from *t* and *u*
16. Diagonal join – mixed
17. Diagonal join to an anticlockwise letter from *a* and *c*
18. Diagonal join to an anticlockwise letter from *d* and *e*
19. Diagonal join to an anticlockwise letter from *h* and *i*
20. Diagonal join to an anticlockwise letter from *k* and *l*
21. Diagonal join to an anticlockwise letter from *m* and *n*
22. Diagonal join to an anticlockwise letter from *t* and *u*
23. All diagonal joins (1)
24. All diagonal joins (2)
25. Horizontal join to ascender from *o* and *w*
26. Horizontal join, no ascender, from *o*
27. Horizontal join, no ascender, from *v* and *w*
28. Horizontal join to an anticlockwise letter from *o*
29. Horizontal join to an anticlockwise letter from *v* and *w*
30. All horizontal joins
31. Joining to ascender and no ascender from *s*
32. Joining to an anticlockwise letter from *s*
33. Joining from *b*
34. Joining from *p*
35. Joining to *f*
36. Joining to and from *f*
37. Joining to ascender and no ascender from *r*
38. Joining to an anticlockwise letter from *r*
39. Practising joined writing (1)
40. Practising joined writing (2)

Book 3 – Securing fluency

1. Keeping closed letters closed – patterns and letter practice
2. Keeping closed letters closed – words
3. Keeping closed letters closed – copying text
4. Keeping closed letters closed – text starter
5. Keeping open letters open – patterns and letter practice
6. Keeping open letters open – words
7. Keeping open letters open – copying text
8. Keeping open letters open – text starter
9. Parallel ascenders and descenders – patterns and letter practice
10. Parallel ascenders and descenders – words
11. Parallel ascenders and descenders – text for copying
12. Parallel ascenders and descenders – text starter
13. Same size x-height letters – patterns and letter practice
14. Same size x-height letters – words
15. Same size x-height letters – text for copying
16. Same size x-height letters – text starter
17. Same height ascenders and capitals – patterns and letter practice
18. Same height ascenders and capitals – words
19. Same height ascenders and capitals – text for copying
20. Same height capitals and ascenders – text starter
21. Keeping ascenders and descenders in proportion – patterns and letter practice
22. Keeping ascenders and descenders in proportion – words
23. Keeping ascenders and descenders in proportion – text for copying
24. Keeping ascenders and descenders in proportion – text starter
25. Regular spaces between letters – patterns and letter practice
26. Regular spaces between letters – words
27. Regular spaces between letters – text for copying
28. Regular spaces between letters – text starter
29. Regular spaces between words – patterns and letter practice
30. Regular spaces between words – words
31. Regular spaces between words – text for copying
32. Regular spaces between words – text starter
33. Regular spaces (all) – patterns and letter practice
34. Regular spaces (all) – words
35. Regular spaces (all) – text for copying
36. Regular spaces (all) – text starter
37. Putting it all together – poem
38. Putting it all together – fiction
39. Putting it all together – instructions
40. Putting it all together – news report

Penpals for Handwriting: Rationale

Traditional principles in the contemporary classroom

We believe that:

1. A flexible, fluent and legible handwriting style empowers children to write with confidence and creativity. This entitlement needs careful progression and skilful, discrete teaching that is frequent and continues beyond the initial foundation stages. The earlier that difficulties can be identified, the easier it is to correct them. The promotion of good handwriting skills requires high-quality teaching.

2. Handwriting is a developmental process with its own distinctive stages of sequential growth. We have identified five stages that form the basic organisational structure of *Penpals*:

   (i) Physical preparation for handwriting: gross and fine motor skills leading to mark-making, patterns and letter formation (Foundation, 3–5 years)

   (ii) Securing correct letter formation (Key Stage 1, 5–6 years)

   (iii) Beginning to join, along with a focus on relative size and spacing (Key Stage 1, 6–7 years)

   (iv) Securing the joins, along with a focus on break letters, legibility, consistency and quality (Lower Key Stage 2, 7–9 years)

   (v) Practising speed, fluency and developing a personalised style for different purposes (Upper Key Stage 2, 9–11 years)

3. Handwriting must also be practised discretely and in context. Beyond the initial foundation stages, *Penpals* provides interactive content with Teacher's Books, Interactives and Practice Books, as well as Workbooks for handwriting practice in the context of age-appropriate spelling, punctuation and grammar. Learning to associate the kinaesthetic handwriting movement with the visual letter pattern and the aural phonemes will help children with learning to spell. However, *Penpals* always takes a 'handwriting first' approach.

4. Choosing the writing implement best suited to the task is an important part of a handwriting education.

A practical approach

Penpals for Handwriting offers a practical, active learning approach to support the delivery of handwriting teaching in response to the increased demands of the National Curriculum 2014.

- **Time:** *Penpals'* focus on whole-class teaching from an interactive whiteboard, with key teaching points clearly identified, allows effective teaching in the time available.
- **Planning:** *Penpals* helps with long-, medium- and short-term planning for each year group, correlated to national guidelines.
- **Practice:** *Penpals* offers pupil Practice Books, as well as Workbooks, with their own internal structure of excellent models for finger tracing, tracing, copying and independent writing.
- **Assessment:** *Penpals* offers many opportunities for assessment, including: self-assessment questions and challenges throughout the Practice Books and Workbooks, two or three assessment units in each year group, and assessment ideas in the Teacher's Books. The *Penpals for Handwriting Intervention Programme* (*Penpals Intervention*) also provides further information, activities and checklists.
- **Motivation:** *Penpals* is attractive and well-designed with clear links between all of the elements in each year group.
- **ICT:** The *Penpals Interactive* enriches and extends.

Differentiation and intervention

In spite of high-quality teaching, some children find handwriting difficult and laborious. The three books in *Penpals Intervention* help support these children:

- *Securing letter formation*: which is intended for children from Year 1 to the end of primary
- *Securing joins*: which is intended for children from Year 3 to the end of primary and into secondary
- *Securing fluency*: which is intended primarily for children from Year 5 until the end of Year 9.

The three books revisit skills which have not transferred into the children's curriculum handwriting. It is not appropriate to use each book with children who are younger than the identified age group for that book because the skills will not yet have been introduced and practised through the main *Penpals* resources.

These books do not replace whole-class teaching with *Penpals*, but can be used for reinforcement or for individual or small group intervention. However, these intervention materials can also be used in schools which do not have *Penpals* as their main handwriting scheme if children have already been introduced to the letter or join in question **and** the handwriting style children have been taught is similar to *Penpals* **and** the adult supporting the intervention can use familiar language to talk about the unit focus.

Penpals for Handwriting Intervention Programme

High-quality teaching will use *Penpals for Handwriting* to teach and apply the new letters or joins and will then use curriculum opportunities for practice. It is important that, once letter formation or joining has been introduced, it is used in all contexts except informal note taking. Children need to know that 'good handwriting' is not something that is only done in handwriting lessons. In addition, it is easier and quicker to teach good pencil grip, posture and formation from the beginning than it is to correct them later on if they have not been used in all situations.

Penpals Intervention is a series of developmentally structured worksheets which introduce letters and the main join types in the same order as the main *Penpals* programme. However, *Penpals Intervention* may present letter combinations within each join type in a different order from the main programme.

While each worksheet can be used as a standalone, it is preferable to use them alongside the relevant unit from the *Penpals Interactives* so that each letter or join can be watched in animated form and then modelled and practised electronically before children begin the worksheet.

The photocopiable activities on the worksheets can be used and revisited as often as necessary, increasing accuracy and speed on each repetition.

The *Penpals Intervention* books are intended to be used in one of four ways:

- **Quick catch-up:** You can use *Penpals Intervention* as a dip-in resource for children who are new to your class or for those who you think need additional practice with some isolated letters or joins. Use the Contents page to find the best worksheet(s) to address the identified problem and supervise the children while they complete the worksheets to ensure that teaching and learning are focused on progress.
- **Support:** During your whole-class *Penpals* lesson, you may have a few children who are not yet ready for the additional opportunities provided in the Workbook. Those children may benefit from additional handwriting practice which can be afforded by the *Penpals Intervention* worksheets. Please note, however, that there is not a unit-to-unit correspondence and some units may be supported by more than one worksheet whereas others may not have any.
- **Reinforcement:** For some children, a few aspects of handwriting need to be reinforced and secured. In these instances, small-group targeted activities from *Penpals Intervention* can be given for reinforcement, supported by an adult.
- **Intervention:** A few children struggle to learn handwriting. Although this may be linked to an identified special need, for most children it is more likely that their muscles were insufficiently developed when handwriting was first introduced so they are constantly playing 'catch-up' and are not ready to move on with their class. The impact of this increases incrementally as children get older. These children will benefit from a more comprehensive one-to-one or small group intervention, supported by an adult.

A few words from the experts

Handwriting is the ultimate fine motor task, which additionally requires skills in hand–eye co-ordination, organisation and sequencing. We expect these skills of very young children, all too often before they are developmentally ready, for example requiring fine motor control of fingers before having postural stability. Pre-writing skills can be learnt, but we should not expect letter and number formation until they can master an oblique cross (X), which requires crossing midline.

Many children with handwriting difficulties are referred to occupational therapists who can help improve letter formation, fluency and pencil grip, for example, but it would be of greater benefit to make sure children get the basics of handwriting correct at the outset. *Penpals for Handwriting* will help establish the right skills at the right time for each child and so make this essential communication tool a pleasure rather than a chore.

Catherine Elsey, Paediatric Occupational Therapist, National Handwriting Association

How to use *Penpals for Handwriting Intervention* Book 2

Before starting work on any intervention or a programme of additional support, it is essential to assess the child's strengths and difficulties during handwriting lessons and in their other curriculum writing. Support for pre- and post-intervention assessment can be found on pages 18–20.

Each worksheet in this book, which focuses on securing joins, targets one letter and joins starting with that letter because the initial letter in a pair determines the type of join needed. All the worksheets follow the same progression so that children are immediately familiar with the task. This gives them the opportunity to experience quick success and, if the join is used successfully, they can move on. Alternatively, children can be asked to repeat the same worksheet activity and improve their performance.

The expectation while using these worksheets is that children are already experienced in writing all of the upper and lower case letters and are proficient in tracing and copying them using correct letter formation. If there are any concerns about individual letter formation, these should be addressed using *Penpals Intervention Book 1: Securing letter formation* before focusing on joins.

Some of the activities on the worksheet can be timed. This:

- gives children a target for improvement for the next time they repeat the worksheet
- helps to build fluency by practising writing at speed
- secures the join – a join that can be written successfully several times, and when under time pressure, is more likely to become secure in curriculum writing and when writing for a real purpose and audience.

For each intervention session:

1. Identify the handwriting focus that needs attention.
2. Select the appropriate worksheet (see the Contents page).
3. Before you begin, read the success criteria from the Checklist at the bottom of the worksheet so children know what is expected of them.

In all of the worksheets in this book, children follow the progression shown here.

Trace and write the joins.
This gives children practice at writing the most commonly used joins. Always encourage children to trace the joins with a focus on fluency, rather than on painstakingly following the exact line. The act of tracing should support the creation of a 'muscle memory'.

Read, trace and write the words.
Again, encourage all children to trace as fluently as possible. However, be alert for letters which are not correctly formed in order to identify next steps. This activity is timed to encourage fast, fluent and legible joining.

Read, trace and write the sentence.
Children should now work independently to make an accurate copy of the words or sentence. Again, this activity is timed.

Self-assess.
Ask the children to evaluate their joins using the criteria in the Checklist. They can then self-assess the overall outcomes and identify the best join or joins.

Example worksheets

Unit 1: Diagonal join to ascender from a

Name _____ Date _____
Trace and write the joins.

al al at at ah ah ab ab ak ak af af

Read, trace and write the words. Time yourself. Write your time here. ( )

walk walk   that that   ahead ahead

about about   cake cake   afraid afraid

Read, trace and write the sentence. Time yourself. Write your time here. ( )

I'm afraid that Hannah ate all of the cake.

Check
☑ Tick the best joins from a.

Checklist!
☐ The letters are equally spaced.
☐ The join from a meets the second letter at about x-height.

Unit 26: Horizontal join to ascender from g and w

Name _____ Date _____
Trace and write the joins.

gh gh gt gt gl gl wb wb wl wl wh wh

Read, trace and write the words. Time yourself. Write your time here. ( )

John John   got got   snowballs snowballs

told told   scowled scowled   when when

Read, trace and write the sentence. Time yourself. Write your time here. ( )

John scowled when he got told not to throw snowballs.

Check
☑ Tick the best joins from o.
☑ Tick the best joins from w.

Checklist
☐ The letters are equally spaced.
☐ All the x-height letters are the same size.
☐ The letters o and w are correctly formed.
☐ The joins from o and w are long enough for the next letter to start in the right place at the top of the ascender.

Introducing joining

Throughout *Penpals for Handwriting*, six different joins are taught and practised:

- diagonal join to ascender (e.g. *at, il, th*)
- diagonal join, no ascender (e.g. *nn, ar, ci*)
- diagonal join to anticlockwise letters (e.g. *ic, eg, dd*)
- horizontal join to ascender (e.g. *ot, wh, rl*)
- horizontal join, no ascender (e.g. *wi, vu, on*)
- horizontal join to anticlockwise letters (e.g. *oo, va, rc*).

The main *Penpals* scheme is cumulative and progressive, so previously learnt joins are practised and reinforced as children progress through the books. For most children, this is good practice because it builds automaticity and secures the muscle memory of previously practised joins. In this intervention book, however, only the focus join is modelled and practised. This is partly because children have different priorities for improvement, so they may access the units in a different order, but mostly because it focuses the child's attention on the specific target join. If children are able to join to and from other letters accurately, they should not be dissuaded from doing so. Keep a careful eye on these other joins to check they are accurate and help to build fluency.

Throughout *Penpals*, new joins, whether diagonal or horizontal, are introduced in the order:

- to ascenders: *b, f, h, k, l, t*
- to no ascenders: *e, i, j, m, n, p, r, u, v, w, y*
- to anticlockwise letters: *a, c, d, g, o, q, s*
- to break letters, which are not joined from: *g, j, y*
- break letters which are not joined to or from: *x* and *z*.

Joins from *r, s,* and *q,* together with joins to and from *f,* are introduced in the *Penpals* Year 3 books. Joins from *b* and *p* are introduced in the *Penpals* Year 4 books.

From the beginning of the *Penpals* Year 3 resources, the assumption is made that children have had sufficient practice in the pencil movements needed for the joins to enable them to transfer their learning to all new combinations of that join. For most children, this transfer is straightforward especially as they will have met many of these joins in the *Penpals* Year 2 resources. Nevertheless, some children benefit from learning and practising each of the most common letter combinations separately.

In this book:

- each of the common letter combinations is taught discretely
- previous experience of other letter pairs joined with the same join can be explicitly discussed and built upon
- the content is organised by considering the initial letter in each pair and looking at how that letter joins to other letters.

The joining letter sets used in this book are shown on the inside back cover.

Handwriting hints: posture and pencil grip

Good posture and a secure and flexible pencil grip become all the more important as the expectation for more sustained curriculum writing increases. By the time they are 7+, some children begin to sit on their feet or to sprawl on the table but they will not be able to write fluently and legibly from that position.

Posture

Good handwriting begins with both feet firmly on the floor so that the downward pressure of the act of writing is balanced evenly between both sides of the body (hips, legs and feet). All the core muscles in the body are necessary if the child is to stay upright and the muscles in the shoulder, arm, wrist, hand and fingers are needed to provide stability and flexibility. In addition, the muscles of the neck are involved to ensure there is no undue discomfort to distract children from their writing.

In order to enable the child to maintain core stability and thus the stability of shoulder, arm, elbow, wrist, hand and fingers, it is important to consider how the child is sitting. If children are sitting with their legs curled up under them or if they are slumped over their work, look at the height of the desk – is it too high or too low for them?

The ideal posture for handwriting is sitting with the feet flat on the floor and the bottom at the back of the seat so that the lower back is supported by the back of the chair. From this position, children should be able to achieve good balance and maintain the core stability upon which all of the other muscles rely.

From that position, encourage children to lean the upper body forwards slightly when they work. This allows them to stabilise their arms and wrists and to rest the outer edge of their hand lightly on the table. The other hand should rest on the table to ensure that the bodyweight is evenly balanced. This hand is often used to hold the paper securely.

Few children work best when the paper is centred directly in front of them as this pushes their elbow into their body and restricts the movement of their wrist and fingers. Let children experiment with the amount of slope which is best for them: right-handers tend to need to slope their paper with a slight lean to the left, so they are writing slightly 'uphill', whereas left-handers may need a steeper slope to the right so they are writing 'downhill'. This allows them to see what they have written.

See the posture poster from the *Penpals Poster Pack*.

Pencil grip

The traditional tripod pencil grip – where the pencil is held loosely between the thumb and forefinger, with the middle finger acting as a stabiliser – is the ideal grip. This is the most flexible grip for both left- and right-handed writers and is most likely to enable fast, sustained writing. Adaptive grips or ergonomic writing tools, and making sure the wrist is stable and the grip is not too tight, will help most children to develop a comfortable handwriting grip.

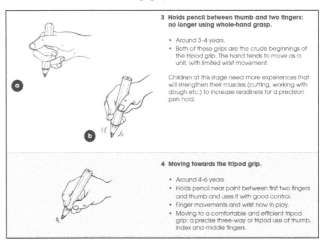

See the pencil hold poster from the *Penpals Poster Pack*.

If children complain of pain when they write, look carefully at the forefinger with which they hold the pencil: both joints should be bent up in the same direction, creating a rough circle between thumb and forefinger. If the first joint of the forefinger is bent down, the child's pencil grip will be too tight with limited flexibility of the fingers. In that position, the movement comes mostly from the hand, wrist and elbow and great tension is placed on the tendons leading down the back of the hand. Also look carefully at wrist position and stability. Hooking the wrist and lifting the wrist away from the table are both likely to impact overall comfort when writing. Time spent correcting these pencil grip difficulties will be time well spent.

Where a less-than-perfect handwriting grip is established but does not cause the writer pain or fatigue and the writing is of average speed and legible, it will be more beneficial to focus on the content of the writing rather than working on optimising the grip.

Alternative grip

If children find it hard to correct a habitual bad grip, offer them an alternative grip. Ask them to place the pencil between the index and middle fingers and direct the movement of the pencil using thumb, index and middle fingers. This grip is sufficiently flexible to enable fluent, pain-free handwriting when bad habits are too entrenched to change.

Potential barriers to good handwriting in children aged 7+

For most children, there is rapid progress in handwriting while letter formation is learned and consolidated during Reception/Primary 1 (ages 4–5), followed by a period of consolidation during Year 1/Primary 2 which may extend into Year 2/Primary 3 (age 7).

The aim is that during Year 3 or 4 / Primary 4 or 5 (ages 8–9) there should be a further phase of swift improvement as handwriting becomes automatic and organised so that it becomes an effective tool for the expression of ideas. Children who are still making slow progress when they are aged 8 or 9, and whose handwriting continues to be laborious, may benefit from swift, effective and targeted intervention.

The most important qualities of 'good' handwriting are legibility and speed. Consistent letter size and spacing play a significant role in the readability of handwriting, and the ability to produce parallel downstrokes on a slight slope impacts on the speed. Underpinning all of this, however, is good letter formation.

There are two broad types of barriers to good handwriting: the physical environment and factors which are internal to the child. See page 9 for a checklist of handwriting difficulties observed as a result of environmental factors, and possible adaptations to try to resolve these difficulties.

The easiest way to discount any of the environmental factors which may contribute to poor handwriting is to ensure that the child has opportunities to write in different physical environments and to compare their handwriting.

Handwriting 'capabilities'

Handwriting is a hugely complex skill which requires a blend of hand–eye co-ordination, the ability to plan how groups of muscles will work together, thinking skills and perceptual skills as well as good tactile and kinaesthetic sensitivities and the ability to sustain attention.

- The development of fine motor skills is the most common barrier to good handwriting, especially in younger children. If fine motor skills were delayed but are now appropriately developed, the child may need to consolidate letter formation using *Penpals Intervention Book 1: Securing letter formation* with sufficient opportunities to practise so that good letter formation becomes automatic.
- Some children find it hard when their right and left hand do not work well together because handwriting involves one hand moving while the other stays still and stabilises the paper. These children tend to either fidget with their non-writing hand or they move their jaw in compensation for not moving that hand.

- Visual–motor integration, also known as hand–eye co-ordination, is an important factor in handwriting. Children who have been drilled to do handwriting before they were ready often turn out to have difficulties with visual–motor integration.
- Children with poor tactile awareness or proprioception (that is, the ability to know where particular body parts are and what they are doing) often find it hard to judge appropriate pressure, with the result that they tend either to press too hard or to have spidery writing. Ask the child to write on three pieces of paper interleaved with two pages of carbon paper. Challenge the child to press hard enough to make one copy of their writing, but not two. Poor proprioception can also result in difficulties with directionality and with writing on baselines.
- Poor sensory awareness in the fingertips can also result in poor handwriting because the child cannot sense small pencil movements. Watch while the child performs the fine motor activities in *Penpals* gym on the *Penpals Interactives* and see whether their fingers are nimble and whether they can use appropriate pressure when pressing against their thumbs.
- Sustained attention is also critical for good handwriting. Many children with ADHD have handwriting which shows inconsistent letter sizes and shapes.

In addition, many common SENDs have implications for handwriting (see pages 14–17). Before you start a handwriting intervention, it is important that you understand what might be causing the child's difficulties. Although many of the same activities will still be appropriate, the targets for the intervention will vary depending on the reason for the difficulty.

Physical environment

Name .... Date ....

LH / RH (circle)   Any other comments ....

Handwriting difficulties observed	Questions to consider	Adaptations to try (circle any selected for the learner)
The child is not sitting with the correct posture, e.g. slumped, too near, too far from desk, sideways to desk, sitting on one foot, kneeling or sprawling on the table.	Has the child developed good posture for handwriting?	Ensure the height of the table and chair are appropriate. Half-line space between this line and line above. Watch the child in PE and sitting on the carpet. Does the child have the muscle strength to sustain the correct posture, or is support required from a specialist such as a physiotherapist or occupational therapist to develop the necessary muscles? Use a wedge-shaped cushion for the child to sit on. This pushes the weight away from the hips and onto the child's feet.
The child is too short for the table or chair. The child is too big for the table or chair.	Are the table and chair at the right height to allow the child to assume the correct posture?	Borrow tables and chairs from other rooms to see what difference they make to the child's posture. Consider using footrests, writing slopes or pencil grips (see page 13).
The child complains that their hand or wrist hurts. The child shakes their hand or wrist. The child rubs or stretches their arm, hand, wrist or fingers.	Are the behaviours observed every time the child writes? Is the pressure used for handwriting appropriate, or is the child pressing too hard?	Look carefully at the forefinger with which the child holds the pencil: both joints should be flexed in the same direction, creating a rough circle between the thumb and forefinger. If the first joint of the forefinger is bent down, the child's pencil grip will be too tight with limited flexibility of the fingers. In that position, the writing movement comes mostly from the hand, wrist and elbow placing great tension on the tendons leading down the back of the hand. Constantly remind the child to form that circle. Check that the wrist is stable and correctly positioned relative to the writing line. This is a common area to address if handwriting causes pain. Pain can also be experienced with a thumb-wrapping grasp where the thumb wraps around the pencil and index finger, resulting in a fist-like grasp which uses the whole hand to write.
Pencils are not well-maintained for lessons. Writing is smudged. Writing is scratched through the paper.	Is the child using an appropriate writing instrument? Is their pencil too hard, too soft, too blunt? Would they benefit from a pencil with better support for grip? Would a pencil grip help (see page 13)?	For some children the typical HB pencil is not an appropriate writing instrument and they may do better with a softer pencil lead. Ballpoint pens are never suitable handwriting tools, but some children will do better with gel pens or felt-tipped pens than with pencils or more traditional handwriting pens.
Writing is squashed. Writing is breaking out of the line guidance.	Are the lines on the paper appropriately spaced for the child to write comfortably?	Making children reduce their natural size of writing too quickly in order to accommodate to a 'class standard' of line spacing in exercise books can result in cramped, uncomfortable writing. Photocopy the line guides on pages 63–64. How does the child's handwriting change when line spacing is increased or decreased?
Writing begins erratically on the page. Writing misses line spaces.	Is the child clear where to start writing and which line to move onto next?	Ensure the child always writes on lined paper, not using line guides which may slip. Mark the left-hand margins with different coloured dots to show where to start writing on each line and also to set up a pattern of colours to follow, e.g. green, red, blue, green, red, blue. If this is still a problem, go over the entire line using a highlighter pen or buy writing paper with raised lines (e.g. Right Line Paper™ from Taskmaster) to give a clear tactile reference.
The child uses classroom posters, a frieze or a working wall for support. The child uses table-top models for support.	Are models of good letter formation in clear view from where the child is sitting?	Ensure there is a card on the table so the child can finger trace letters to reinforce orientation. Learning to join should also support these children.
The child sits awkwardly. Argues with child sitting next to them. Paper and pencils fall frequently from the desk.	Is there space for the child to tilt their paper to an appropriate angle? Is there enough elbow room?	Offer a writing mat with guidelines for tilt, or stick tape on the table to model the tilt. Do not position a left-handed child to the right of a right-handed child, and vice versa, or their elbows will knock and they risk becoming cramped writers.
The child complains of headaches when writing. They find it hard to write on the lines. They sit with their nose too close to the paper.	What is the lighting like where the child is sitting? Is it too harsh or too dim? Does the child have a sensitivity to the high-frequency flicker of fluorescent lights?	Illuminating the child's workspace with an ordinary desk lamp can minimise the impact of this.
The child looks up frequently. The child makes frequent excuses to move around the classroom or attract attention.	Are there other classroom distractions such as noise or movement?	Consider providing a desktop privacy screen. Sit the child facing the board, away from distractions provided by other children.
The child is reluctant to start writing tasks. Writing activities are rarely finished. The child becomes frustrated after a short time of writing.	How much handwriting is the child expected to complete?	Differentiating quantity in favour of quality in the short term should lead to improved outcomes in the longer term.

Handwriting hints: supporting left-handed writers

At least ten per cent of the population are left-handed. Being left-handed should not be used as an excuse for poor handwriting: with appropriate support, left-handed children have the same capacity for efficient and fluent handwriting as their right-handed peers. However, it is important to remember that teaching left-handed children to write does not simply involve asking them to mirror what right-handed children are doing. The four most important things to be aware of are:

- the position of the exercise book or paper
- the position of the arm and the wrist
- the pencil grip
- the ability to visually monitor the pencil point.

Unless these are considered, many left-handed people adopt a writing position in which they hook their hand around and above the line of text. This is cramped, uncomfortable and difficult to sustain for any length of time.

Left-handed children will particularly benefit from large-scale mark-making activities using chalk, marker pens, paint-brushes, fingers, sticks and so on (see *Penpals F1 Teacher's Book*). These children may need to have access to these activities for longer than their right-handed peers while they learn to make letter shapes using big, whole-arm motions.

The position of the exercise book or paper relative to the position of the arm and the wrist

Right-handed children *pull* the pencil across the paper from left to right so they can always see what they have written. Left-handed children *push* the pencil across the paper from left to right so their hand tends to cover up their writing. In order to avoid this, left-handed writers need to tilt their books at a more acute angle than right-handed writers.

Left-handed children should place the paper to the left of their midline and slope the paper so that they are writing 'downhill' towards themselves, without covering what they have just written.

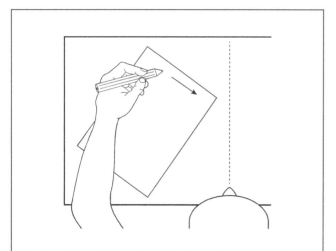

- Ask these children to place their arm on the table in the position they use to write.
- Line up the vertical edges of their paper to be parallel with their forearm, and then slightly increase the slope.

The 'correct' angle will be different for all children, and some may even prefer not to have a tilted page; but teaching them with this level of tilted page from the beginning will help them to become accustomed to it. Ensure that the hand which stabilises the paper is below where the children are writing, or is well above it as the writer moves towards the bottom of the page.

Pencil grip

Whereas right-handed children will often hold their pencil at about 1-1.5 cm from the point, left-handed children should be encouraged to hold the pencil slightly further from the point so that they can see what they have written. You may wish to place a soft pencil grip at this distance from the point until the child automatically holds the pencil at this distance.

The tripod pencil grip (see the *Penpals Poster Pack* and education.cambridge.org/Penpals) is the most flexible grip for both left- and right-handed writers and is most likely to enable fast, fluent and sustained writing. The alternative grip described on page 7 is equally appropriate for left-handed children.

Handwriting hints: keeping handwriting 'neat', legible and presentable

When we ask children to do 'neat' handwriting, they often do not seem sure about what precisely we mean and what constitutes 'neat' handwriting. The components for neat, legible and presentable handwriting are generally agreed to be:

- good letter formation
- accurate joins
- consistent size of x-height letters
- length of ascenders and descenders in proportion to x-height letters: letters with ascenders are twice the height of x-height letters (so *l* is twice the height of *i*); descenders are as deep as x-height letters are tall (so the tail on *y* hangs the same depth below the line as *u* is above it); letter *t* is slightly shorter than other ascenders.
- consistent spaces between letters in a word
- consistent spaces between words – between one and two letter *o* spaces
- all downstrokes are parallel including ascenders, descenders and downstrokes on x-height letters.

Breaking down 'neat' handwriting into these components is often easier for children. Negotiate some 'rules for neat handwriting' in the class or group of children and refer to them as often as necessary. As for many complex tasks, children may benefit from focusing on one aspect of neat handwriting at a time.

TIPS

Encouraging neat handwriting

- Allow children to use an individual whiteboard to reinforce joins in common words. Teach the child to trace–wipe–write:
  - You write the word or join.
  - The child traces it.
  - The child wipes off their writing (by putting a cloth over the end of their pen and retracing the writing to rub it out).
  - The child writes the word or join.
- Emphasise that accurate joining is necessary to maintain consistent spacing as the length of the join determines the spacing.
- Use handwriting paper with horizontal 'tramlines' (see page 63) to practise the height of ascenders and the length of descenders.
- Use handwriting paper with 'guidelines' to show the appropriate angle for downstrokes (see page 64) to practise keeping all downstrokes parallel.
- Ask the child to write using 5 mm squared paper (which shows x-height) to keep spacing consistent.

Finger spacing

Avoid the use of fingers to show 'finger spacing' between words because:

- it slows the flow of the writing if children need to keep on placing their finger on the page
- it is particularly disruptive for left-handed children
- children should be encouraged to use their 'free' hand to stabilise their paper, which they cannot do if that hand is constantly being called upon for spacing
- children's posture is always shifting if they keep placing their free hand at different points on the line, so it becomes more and more difficult to sustain parallel downstrokes
- by the time children are 7+, their fingers are generally too broad so the spacing is too wide and finger size also varies. *Penpals for Handwriting* advocates leaving about two letter *o*s of a child's writing between words.

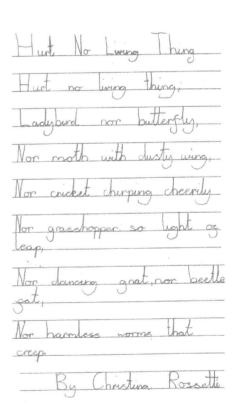

Handwriting hints: building up speed, fluency and legibility

The need to write at speed, while maintaining legibility, is one of the key aims of learning handwriting. As children progress through school, they are asked to write across the curriculum for increased periods of time and for an increasing range of purposes. They need to be able to:

- write without having to think about the formation of letters and spelling so as to focus entirely on the content of their writing
- write neatly and carefully for presentation and display
- write in a fast, fluent and legible manner for writing stories, information reports, letters, biographies, journalistic articles, instructions, advertisements, arguments or other curriculum purposes
- write notes for planning, for recording ideas, for gathering information, for lists or other curriculum purposes.

The main *Penpals* resource provides children with the opportunity to experience all these different types and purposes for writing and encourages older children to develop their own, individual and comfortable style for sustained writing.

Building speed

The focus in this book is on developing fast, fluent and legible handwriting. This is achieved by giving children opportunities to copy words and sentences slowly and then at an increased speed without losing legibility or 'neatness'. This approach supports children because:

- there are no additional cognitive demands – after the child has written the text once, additional reiterations simply provide copying practice
- all texts for copying are short so all children should be able to maintain focus while they are copying
- the children are expected to self-assess – this means they are constantly teaching themselves about what is 'good' and what needs to be improved, so they do not start to compromise the quality of their handwriting as they build up the speed
- they copy the same join over and over which means that the hand movement needed for the join begins to become automatic and muscle memory is created and reinforced.

The aim is to build 'automaticity': if the join becomes automatic, the child does not need to think about it but just writes it accurately and as often as necessary.

TIPS

Non-handwriting activities to build fluency
- Give children ribbons to make big joining movements in the air while watching the ribbons flowing.
- Let children try creating two-handed big and flowing patterns on a whiteboard or on both sides of a board simultaneously.
- Give children paintbrushes and water to draw big patterns of joined up letters.
- Encourage children to make flowing patterns in time to music.
- Make flowing patterns between two lines, touching both top and bottom lines. The patterns should be about four to five repetitions to mimic word length.

Handwriting hints: using pencil grips, ergonomic pencils and writing slopes

Various pencil grips are available to meet a range of difficulties. So, before you prescribe a generic pencil grip, consider what the problem is and how old the child is, since as they get older some children become embarrassed by using pencil grips.

Improving the grip

Improving the tripod grip is the most common reason for offering a child a pencil grip. A range of options are available.

- The most traditional pencil grip is a triangular prism-shape which you push onto a pencil. Many children find it hard to sustain writing with these grips as they are not shaped to accommodate fingers.

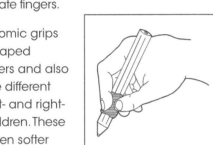

- More ergonomic grips are often shaped around fingers and also allow for the different needs of left- and right-handed children. These grips are often softer to relieve tension and fatigue while reinforcing a good tripod grip. These grips often come with 'wings' to prevent fingers and thumbs from overlapping and crossing over each other.

- The writing 'claw', which is a grip with three horizontal cups to accommodate finger tips, is good for supporting younger children who are just discovering a tripod grip.

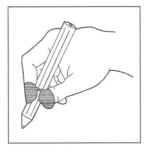

Relieving tension and providing sensory feedback

For slightly older children, there are a range of textured and padded grips that can both reduce strain if children are holding the pencil too tightly and give increased control to children who benefit from clear sensory feedback.

As we write, our hands tend to slip down the barrel of the writing instrument, causing us to grip harder, which in turn puts pressure on the tendons in the hand. Grips can be used to reduce the slippage.

- Soft grips, which are made from tubes of foam or silicon, can help to relieve tension and fatigue caused by gripping a pencil too tightly. These are ideal for older children whose pencil grip is broadly adequate but whose hands get tired writing.
- Textured grips, which are usually made from gel or silicone tubes, give particular support to children who need tactile feedback. These can be slightly shaped to stabilise fingers.

Ergonomic pencils

In addition to pencil grips, which can be transferred to different writing and colouring implements, you can now buy ergonomic pens and pencils. At the simplest level, these are simply triangular shaped to encourage the use of a tripod grip. However, most of these writing implements are now moulded to encourage the correct grip. Many brands also supply various designs to accommodate different-sized hands and the different stages children progress through as they develop an automatic and comfortable tripod grip.

Writing slopes

Some children benefit from using a writing slope or board because the use of the slope reduces strain on the neck, back, shoulders and eyes. If a child is experiencing any difficulties with writing, it is worth exploring the use of a writing slope. Ideally, buy one with a non-slip surface or put a non-slip cover onto the slope. You may also need a non-slip cover on the desk or table where the child will be sitting to ensure that the slope stays still.

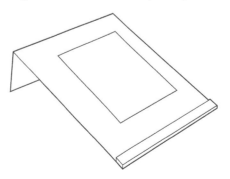

Writing slopes are particularly useful for:

- left-handed children
- children with dyslexia
- children with a developmental co-ordination disorder (DCD)/dyspraxia.

SEN and handwriting: visual perception

While handwriting is primarily a motor skill, it is also a visual skill and requires children to process a lot of visual information. The aim is that the look or sound of a letter should subconsciously and immediately trigger a motor response. This deals with the shape of the letter, but visual perception is also needed to ensure that a sequence of letters sits on the baseline and that the letters are correctly orientated, consistently sized and reasonably spaced.

Visual perception is not a difficulty with the eye that can be corrected by spectacles: rather it is a difficulty in how the brain interprets the signals sent by the eye. Children with visual perception difficulties may experience a range of problems, depending on the nature of their difficulty. They may, for example, experience problems with:

- remembering information presented visually (e.g. that the visual letter form *m* represents the sound /m/)
- remembering the order of things (e.g. that the stick of an *r* comes before the curve)
- identifying a letter when it is only partly visible or in an unfamiliar colour or context
- understanding that shapes such as a a *a* @ *a* a can all be variations of the same letter
- identifying one letter shape in a line or focusing on one part of a busy page
- knowing that a letter sitting on a baseline is the same letter as the letter without a baseline (i.e. that *a* is the same letter as *a*)
- copying a sequence of letters in order
- orientating letters consistently
- perceiving where a pencil mark is in relation to their body and to other pencil marks
- recognising key features which distinguish similar looking letters (e.g. the length of the upright line for *n* and *h*, the number of curves for *n* and *m*, the length of the curve for *n* and *r*).

If you think a child may have visual difficulties, it is always worth asking their parents to take them for a vision test to check that each eye is able to see separately. If problems persist, you could ask for a referral to a registered behavioural optometrist who will look at how well the child's eyes work together. In addition to these physical aspects of the eye, many optometrists will also consider visual perception.

You can also try to find ways to work around visual perception difficulties. For example:

- Allow the child to write on off-white paper and whiteboards.
- Darken, colour or highlight the baseline.
- Teach the letter patters (see *Penpals F2 Teacher's Book*) while forming the letters.

- Spend additional time on reinforcing letter formation using different media, different sizes of writing implement or writing with eyes closed (see *Penpals F1 Teacher's Book* for additional ideas).
- Encourage tracing and overwriting of adult letters to reinforce the kinaesthetic movement.
- Use a coloured dot at the beginning of a line for writing and a different coloured dot at the end so that the child knows where to start and finish.
- Use squared paper and ask the child to write one letter inside each square.
- Use a masking device so that only the letter to be copied is visible on the page.
- Let the child try using a writing slope.
- Try sensory paper which has raised lines so the child can feel them.
- Consider different types of rubber pencil grip to give different kinaesthetic feedback to the child.
- Allow the child to handle and match magnetic and tactile letters.
- Encourage the use of the *Penpals* alphabet (see *Interactives*), which uses animations to show correct letter formation.

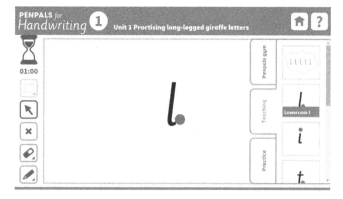

- Give the child opportunities to use the *Penpals Interactives* on-screen tools to explore the activities on the *Penpals* F1 Creative Mark-making Interactive.
- Teach the child how to use self-assessment to improve their own writing.

Above all, be flexible and explore options with the child. There is no 'one-size-fits-all' approach and time spent supporting a child with visual perception difficulties now will save a lot of frustration later.

SEN and handwriting: working memory

Poor working memory is linked to many developmental difficulties including ADHD and dyslexia as well as other difficulties linked to the acquisition of reading, writing and numeracy. Memory difficulties can also occur without any other condition and can continue to threaten a child's educational progress.

What is working memory?
It is the information we hold in our heads for just a few seconds while we do something with it.

Why is working memory important for handwriting?
For children to copy a letter shape or a join or a word, we need them to look at the model, remember it and then focus their eyes on the copy they are making. Children with poor working memory, particularly visual working memory, find it hard to retain the image while they make their own copy of it.

Can it be trained?
The answer to this is still not clear, despite much debate. The evidence is that children become better at doing what they have been explicitly taught to do, but may not be able to transfer that understanding to new ideas or information (see www.york.ac.uk/res/wml/Classroom%20guide.pdf). However, we do know that children improve at what they have been explicitly taught and that 'overlearning' (that is, practising something until it becomes embedded in long-term memory) is effective at supporting children with weak working memories (see http://andrewvs.blogs.com/usu/files/effect_of_overlearning_on_retention.pdf).

What are the implications for phonics and spelling?
Using a multi-sensory approach (which gives lots of mutually supportive memory threads) is effective in embedding ideas in long-term memory, so an approach to phonics and spelling which involves children simultaneously seeing the sound or word, saying the sound or word and creating a muscle memory of the sound or word is an effective way to teach and reinforce phonics and spelling.

What are the implications for handwriting?
A child with weak working memory is likely to need additional practice at forming each of the main handwriting joins and then at transferring what they have learned about one join (e.g. *al*) to another (e.g. *at*). These children will need more practice than their peers in all aspects of handwriting.

The aim of the *Penpals Intervention* books is to give children as many additional opportunities to practise accurate letter formation and joining as they need, while experiencing all the common letter combinations for which each join is required. This practice should allow children to create and consolidate muscle memories, reinforced by visual and auditory memories. You can provide practice opportunities by using the worksheets in this book in school and at home as often as necessary – always involving the children in assessing their progress, appreciating their strengths and identifying points for development.

Throughout all the *Penpals* resources, children are given additional opportunities for developing memory for handwriting through:

- multi-sensory activities as described in the *Penpals F1 Teacher's Book* – Creative Mark-making and the corresponding Interactive
- animations of all letter formations and some joins, which can be mirrored through skywriting, writing with a finger on another child's back or on your own palm, or writing with a marker pen on a whiteboard

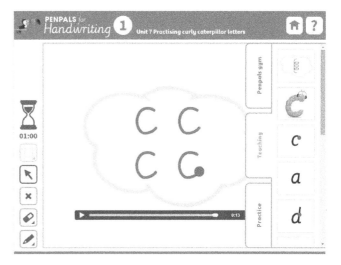

- using the *Penpals* letter patters from the *Penpals F2 Teacher's Book* to describe the pencil movements while writing each letter

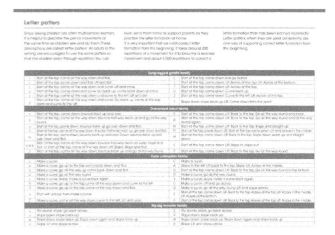

- learning each join in a range of contexts, thus building on what is already known and familiar
- using the *Penpals* Notepad or any of the *Penpals Interactives* for writing pairs of letters in different colours and at different sizes.

SEN and handwriting: handwriting difficulties and dyslexia

Dyslexia, developmental co-ordination disorder (DCD)/ dyspraxia, autism and AD(H)D are among the most common of the specific learning difficulties (SpLD) we encounter in our classrooms. In addition to their primary symptoms, all children with specific learning difficulties are at risk from:

- weak language development and social skills
- low self-esteem
- poor organisation and sequencing skills
- working memory difficulties
- limited concentration
- perceptual and sensory processing difficulties (visual, auditory, proprioceptive).

Not all children experience all of these difficulties, but all children with a SpLD will experience some of them – and all of these difficulties impact on handwriting. Some children with dyslexia have trouble with reading, and often writing, whereas others just have difficulties with writing: spelling, grammar, handwriting, planning and organising ideas.

All classroom accommodations for dyslexic children will also support children with handwriting difficulties.

- Ensure the writing environment is appropriate for the child (see page 9 for more information).
- Check that the child has easy access to stage-appropriate desktop support. If necessary, try creating an A5 ring-binder which the child can personalise but which contains pages to support letter formation, reminders about letter orientation, joins, spacing between letters, rules for 'neat handwriting', spelling, word banks and punctuation hints as well as visual support for organisation, memory, concentration and so on.
- Allow additional time for all activities involving writing.
- Create topic-specific word banks with the child before they write and then leave these with them while they are writing.
- Teach planning skills very thoroughly and allow partner work while planning.
- Provide writing frames which give organisational hints as well as creating smaller spaces for the child to fill.
- Ensure that the child has talked through the content of the piece before they write. Try teaching them to 'talk with a writer', using a silly voice, so they talk to their plan, rehearsing the phrase and sentence structures they intend to write.
- Allow them to use simple recording devices (many of which can now have headphones attached) so they orally record a sentence, a paragraph or a piece of text and then play it back while they write. This removes the need to compose text at the same time as transcribing it

and enables the child to focus on handwriting, spelling and punctuation.
- Create proofreading challenges where you break down the task into 20-second segments and ask children to spot and correct, for example, five spelling mistakes and three punctuation errors and identify one sentence to improve.
- Put green dots in the margins beside every other line and ask children only to write on these lines. This allows them to correct and improve their handwriting or spelling or sentence structures without making the page messy.

The most important tool for developing handwriting across the curriculum will always be self-assessment to identify what went well in addition to what needs to be improved. Use the model suggested in the *main Penpals* programme:

- Find two words to tick.
- Find two words to improve and write them.

Constant reinforcement of the main ideas for good handwriting (accurate letter formation and joining, spacing within and between words, consistent size and proportion, and parallel downstrokes), together with consistently high expectations for handwriting and presentation, will support all children in improving and maintaining progress. If untidy handwriting is accepted because the content is good, children will recognise that handwriting is not the priority and so it will cease to be a priority for them.

Many children with dyslexia and handwriting difficulties will eventually benefit from the opportunity to use ICT to support them for substantive pieces of writing, although shorter tasks such as comprehension activities should generally be completed using handwriting. Another useful tool is a programme which can be made to include banks of words, sentence frames, pictures and sound effects, and can also read back what the child has written. However, the expectation remains that most children should be able to produce fast, fluent and legible handwriting in spite of any underlying difficulties.

SEN and handwriting: DCD/dyspraxia

Weak handwriting is one of the primary symptoms of DCD, which is the internationally accepted name for the more familiar developmental dyspraxia. Children with DCD can have:

- poor fine (and often gross) motor control
- visual perception difficulties
- difficulties with ideation, organisation and sequencing
- difficulties with motor planning.

These are all key skills needed for good handwriting. One of the most frustrating aspects of working with children with DCD is that their performance and their 'ability' varies from day to day and sometimes from hour to hour. Sometimes something taught on day 1, which seems to have been grasped on day 2, appears to have been forgotten on day 3 ... which is frustrating for both the child and the teacher. Since handwriting is so often the way we invite children to share their opinions and express themselves at primary school and since it is increasingly a curriculum necessity, poor handwriting is increasingly linked to poor self-esteem.

If you think a child may have DCD/dyspraxia, refer them for assessment and diagnosis to a paediatrician or occupational therapist, depending on your local referral pathway. In the meantime, you can consider ways of differentiating to meet the needs you have identified. Ways to support children with indications of DCD often overlap with the physical environment issues and handwriting capabilities discussed on pages 8–9 and the ideas offered to support children with dyslexia and handwriting difficulties on page 16.

- Check posture. Is the table at the child's seated elbow height? (See page 7 for more ideas.)
- Check tilt or angle of paper. (See page 9 for more ideas.)
- Check for pencil pressure. (See page 13 for more ideas.)
- Make sure the child consistently uses a relaxed pencil grip with appropriate tension and wrist support.
- Try using dots in the margins or raised line paper so the child knows which line to write on

and has a better chance of staying on the line. (See page 13 for more ideas.)
- Try using a pencil grip or ergonomic pencil. (See page 13 for more ideas.)
- Try using a writing slope. (See page 13 for more ideas.)

In addition, it is helpful to address some of the factors which contribute to poor handwriting (see page 13).

Fine motor skills

There is no doubt that children whose fine motor skills continue to lag behind their peers' will have difficulties with handwriting. Fine motor skills activities used in the EYFS (such as playdough and bead-threading) would continue to be beneficial for these children but, to avoid making the children feel patronised, we need to find ways to focus on the same skills but in age-appropriate contexts. For example:

- Amend dot-to-dot activities so that children are joining letters of the alphabet, counting in twos, etc.
- Create opportunities for games which need fine motor skills like pick-up-sticks, tiddlywinks, Jenga™, Buckaroo™ and Operation™.
- Teach children to sew buttons onto pieces of felt or to learn cross-stitching using Binka™. Reinforce number bonds or times tables while teaching curve-stitching. Or teach the children to knit.
- Provide opportunities for children to cut out increasingly complex shapes, linked to your curriculum.
- Use mathematical construction toys or geoboards to reinforce shape or use pegboards for symmetry, co-ordinates or statistics/data handling.
- Encourage the use of other classroom construction toys.
- Start a Lego™ Therapy Group to enhance social skills as well as fine motor skills.
- Make maximum use of creative opportunities across the curriculum and involve the children in lots of activities which build fine motor skills or strengthen the fingers.

Using the assessments in *Penpals Intervention*

Assessment overview (page 18): Before you decide how to use the *Penpals Intervention* resources, and which book to use, it is vital to gather information about the child.

Handwriting assessment: checking letter formation (page 19): Use this to identify any letters which need to be targeted.

Handwriting assessment: checking joins (page 20): Use this checklist before and after an intervention to identify the specific join or joins which need support or remediation.

Assessment overview

Child's name _____ Date _____

School year _____ Teacher/Form _____

Known SEN: ✔ for confirmed diagnosis; **?** for 'shows characteristics of' or suspected/unconfirmed diagnosis

❑ dyslexia   ❑ dyspraxia/DCD   ❑ autism/Asperger's syndrome
❑ ADHD   ❑ sensory disorders   ❑ hearing impairment
❑ speech/language needs   ❑ social/emotional/mental health   ❑ visual impairment
❑ cerebral palsy   ❑ Down's syndrome   ❑ learning difficulties
❑ other (specify) _____

Handwriting analysis completed by _____ using:

❑ handwriting book   ❑ English/literacy book   ❑ cross-curricular books
❑ other (specify) _____

Dominant hand   ❑ right   ❑ left   ❑ undecided

Please comment on each aspect of handwriting:

Aspect of handwriting	1 = intervention needed, 2 = support needed, 3 = some concern, 4 = no concern				**Comment** (list any letters or joins that cause concern)
	1	2	3	4	
Pencil grip					
Wrist stability					
Pressure					
Paper position					
Keeping to the line					
Posture for handwriting					
Letter formation					
Joins					
Spacing between letters					
Spacing between words					
Consistent size					
Consistent proportion					
Parallel downstrokes					
Fluency and evenness of pencil strokes					
Writing at speed					
Actions to be taken following handwriting analysis:					

Handwriting assessment: checking letter formation

Child's name _____ Date _____

School year _____ Teacher/Form _____

Handwriting analysis completed by _____

- Evaluate each letter individually, in each of the contexts specified.
- Look for at least six repetitions in each of the different contexts in as many different books as possible.
- Record ✔ if the letter is generally appropriate, ? if there are some errors and ✱ if you have concerns.

Letter	In isolation	Consistent orientation	In copied words	In copied text	In independent words	In independent text	Consistent size	Consistent proportion	Downstrokes at appropriate angle	Written at speed	Capital
a											
b											
c											
d											
e											
f											
g											
h											
i											
j											
k											
l											
m											
n											
o											
p											
q											
r											
s											
t											
u											
v											
w											
x											
y											
z											

Handwriting assessment: checking joins

Child's name _____ Date _____

School year _____ Teacher/Form _____

Handwriting analysis completed by _____

- Evaluate each type of join in each of the contexts specified.
- Look for at least six repetitions in each of the different contexts in as many different books as possible.
- Record ✓ if the join is generally appropriate, ? if there are some errors and ✗ if you have concerns.

Type of join	Accuracy in copied text	Accuracy in independent text	Accuracy at speed	Spacing between letters in copied text	Spacing between words in independent text	Spacing between letters at speed	Spacing between words at speed	Parallel downstrokes maintained in copied text	Parallel downstrokes maintained in independent text	Parallel downstrokes maintained at speed
Diagonal join to ascender e.g. *il, tt, nk, ab*										
Diagonal join, no ascender e.g. *ar, ei, up, nn*										
Diagonal join to anticlockwise e.g. *as, ea, ic, lo*										
Horizontal join to ascender e.g. *ob, ol, wh, rk*										
Horizontal join, no ascender e.g. *wi, ve, on, rr*										
Horizontal join to anticlockwise e.g. *rc, wa, fa, oo*										
Join from *b, p* and *s*										
Join to and from *f*										

Child assessment sheet

Name .... Date ....

Before the intervention

I am good at writing these letters:

_____

I sometimes need help with these letters:

_____

After the intervention

Letters	My self-assessment is:	My comments are:
	1 2 3	
	1 2 3	
	1 2 3	
	1 2 3	
	1 2 3	
	1 2 3	
	1 2 3	
	1 2 3	

Next, I want to improve my handwriting by:

_____

_____

_____

Name .... Date ....

Trace and write the joins.

al   al   at   at   ah   ah   ab   ab   ak   ak   af   af

_____

Read, trace and write the words. Time yourself. Write your time here. ⬭

walk   walk   *that   that*   *ahead   ahead*

_____   _____   _____

about   about   *cake   cake*   *afraid   afraid*

_____   _____   _____

Read, trace and write the sentence. Time yourself. Write your time here. ⬭

I'm afraid that Hannah ate all of the cake.

_____

_____

Check
☑ Tick the best joins from *a*.

Checklist
☐ The letters are equally spaced.
☐ The join from *a* meets the second letter at about x-height.

Name .... Date ....

Trace and write the joins.

ck   ck   ch   ch   cl   cl   ct   ct

_____

Read, trace and write the words. Time yourself. Write your time here. ⬭

click click   chicken chicken   children children

_____   _____   _____

class class   octopus octopus   fact fact

_____   _____   _____

Read, trace and write the sentence. Time yourself. Write your time here. ⬭

The class of children found octopus facts.

_____

_____

Check
☑ Tick the best joins from c.

Checklist
☐   The letters are equally spaced.
☐   The join from c is about halfway up the ascender of
     the next letter.

Name _____ Date _____

Trace and write the joins.

el   el   eh   eh   eb   eb   ek   ek   ef   ef

_____

Read, trace and write the words. Time yourself. Write your time here. ⬭

celebrity celebrity   week week   behind behind

_____   _____   _____

cobweb cobweb   basket basket   belief belief

_____   _____   _____

Read, trace and write the sentence. Time yourself. Write your time here. ⬭

The chef felt better when the cobwebs were

removed weekly.

_____

_____

Check
☑ Tick the best joins from *e*.

Checklist
☐ The letters are equally spaced.
☐ The join from *e* is about halfway up the ascender of the next letter.
☐ All the x-height letters are the same size.

Name .... Date ....

Trace and write the joins.

hl hl ht ht ib ib ik ik it it if if

Read, trace and write the words. Time yourself. Write your time here.

athlete athlete   might might   ribbon ribbon

like like   faithful faithful   beautiful beautiful

Read, trace and write the sentence. Time yourself. Write your time here.

Faithful fans waved ribbons at the athletes.

Check
☑ Tick the best joins from *h*.
☑ Tick the best joins from *i*.

Checklist
☐ The letters are equally spaced.
☐ The join from *h* or *i* is about halfway up the ascender of the next letter.

Name .... Date ....

Trace and write the joins.

kf   kf   kh   kh   kl   kl   lt   lt   lf   lf   lb   lb

_____

Read, trace and write the words. Time yourself. Write your time here. ⬭

breakfast breakfast   spilt spilt   ankle ankle

_____   _____   _____

backhand backhand   herself herself   elbow elbow

_____   _____   _____

Read, trace and write the sentence. Time yourself. Write your time here. ⬭

The girl knocked her elbow and spilt her

breakfast.

_____

_____

Check
☑ Tick the best joins from *k*.
☑ Tick the best joins from *l*.

Checklist
☐ The letters are equally spaced.
☐ The ascenders are the same height – except for *t* which is slightly shorter.
☐ The ascenders are parallel.

Name ....   Date ....

Trace and write the joins.

ml   ml   mb   mb   mf   mf   nk   nk   nt   nt   nh   nh

Read, trace and write the words. Time yourself. Write your time here. ⬭

calmly calmly   thanked thanked   comfort comfort

thumbprint   document   unhappy

Read, trace and write the sentence. Time yourself. Write your time here. ⬭

He calmly made thumbprints on the document.

Check
☑ Tick the best joins from *m*.
☑ Tick the best joins from *n*.

Checklist
☐ The letters are equally spaced.
☐ The ascenders are the same height, except for *t* which is slightly shorter.
☐ The joins from *m* or *n* are about halfway up the ascender of the next letter.

Name .... Date ....

Trace and write the joins.

th th tt tt tl tl ttl ttl ub ub ut ut ul ul

_____

Read, trace and write the words. Time yourself. Write your time here. ⬭

with with   the the   beautiful beautiful

_____ _____ _____

rub rub   mouthful mouthful   bottle bottle

_____ _____ _____

Read, trace and write the sentence. Time yourself. Write your time here. ⬭

He settled the beautiful baby with a rub and a

bottle.

_____

_____

Check
☑ Tick the best joins from *t*.
☑ Tick the best joins from *u*.

Checklist
☐ The letters are equally spaced.
☐ The ascenders are the same height, except for *t* which is slightly shorter.
☐ The joins from *t* or *u* are about halfway up the ascender of the next letter.

Name .... Date ....

Trace and write the joins.

ai ai an an ap ap ar ar au au aw aw am am

Read, trace and write the words. Time yourself. Write your time here.

armchair armchair afar afar ambulance ambulance

autograph autograph appear appear await await

Read, trace and write the sentence. Time yourself. Write your time here.

We saw an ambulance appear from afar.

Check
☑ Tick the best joins from *a*.

Checklist
☐ The letters are equally spaced.
☐ All the x-height letters are the same size.
☐ The *a* is correctly formed.

Name .... Date ....

Trace and write the joins.

cr   cr   cu   cu   cy   cy   di   di   dn   dn   dp   dp

Read, trace and write the words. Time yourself. Write your time here. ⬭

crayon crayon   curious curious   cycle cycle

diary diary   didn't didn't   grandpa grandpa

Read, trace and write the sentence. Time yourself. Write your time here. ⬭

Grandpa's curious diary was scribbled in crayon.

Check
☑ Tick the best joins from *c*.
☑ Tick the best joins from *d*.

Checklist
☐ The letters are equally spaced.
☐ All the x-height letters are the same size.
☐ The letters *c* and *d* are correctly formed.

Name .... Date ....

Trace and write the joins.

_ei_   _ei_   _ev_   _ev_   _ew_   _ew_   _er_   _er_   _eu_   _eu_   _ey_   _ey_

Read, trace and write the words. Time yourself. Write your time here. ⬭

their   their   _every   every_   _knew   knew_

where   where   _museum   museum_   _they   they_

Read, trace and write the sentence. Time yourself. Write your time here. ⬭

They knew where everything was in their

museum.

Check
☑ Tick the best joins from _e_.

Checklist
☐ The letters are equally spaced.
☐ All the x-height letters are the same size.
☐ The letter _e_ is correctly formed.

Name .... Date ....

Trace and write the joins.

he he hi hi hr hr ie ie ip ip iv iv

_____

Read, trace and write the words. Time yourself. Write your time here. ⬭

she she   *third third*   *diet diet*

_____   _____   _____

pies pies   *dip dip*   *thrives thrives*

_____   _____   _____

Read, trace and write the sentence. Time yourself. Write your time here. ⬭

She thrives on a diet of pies dipped in ketchup.

_____

_____

Check
☑ Tick the best joins from *h*.
☑ Tick the best joins from *i*.

Checklist
☐ The letters are equally spaced.
☐ All the x-height letters are the same size.
☐ All the ascenders are the same height.
☐ The letters *h* and *i* are correctly formed.

Name .... Date ....

Trace and write the joins.

kn   kn   ki   ki   kp   kp   ke   ke   li   li   lw   lw

_____

Read, trace and write the words. Time yourself. Write your time here. ⬭

know know   liked liked   backpack backpack

_____   _____   _____

cycling cycling   walking walking   always always

_____   _____   _____

Read, trace and write the sentence. Time yourself. Write your time here. ⬭

She always liked walking better than cycling.

_____

_____

Check
☑ Tick the best joins from *k*.
☑ Tick the best joins from *l*.

Checklist
☐ The letters are equally spaced.
☐ All the x-height letters are the same size.
☐ All the ascenders are the same height.
☐ The letter *k* is correctly formed, with the curve at x-height.

Name .... Date ....

Trace and write the joins.

mp mp mm mm my my nr nr ne ne nn nn

_____

Read, trace and write the words. Time yourself. Write your time here. ⬭

never never   summer summer   dreamy dreamy

_____   _____   _____

sunrise sunrise   grumpy grumpy   running running

_____   _____   _____

Read, trace and write the sentence. Time yourself. Write your time here. ⬭

I'm never grumpy when I go running at sunrise.

_____

_____

Check
☑ Tick the best joins from _m_.
☑ Tick the best joins from _n_.

Checklist
☐ The letters are equally spaced.
☐ All the x-height letters are the same size.
☐ The letters _m_ and _n_ are correctly formed, with bridges the same height.

Name .... Date ....

Trace and write the joins.

qu　　qu　　qu　　qu　　qu　　qu　　qu　　qu

Read, trace and write the words. Time yourself. Write your time here. ⬭

quarrel quarrel　　queen queen　　quickly quickly

squirrel squirrel　　quietly quietly　　liquid liquid

Read, trace and write the sentence. Time yourself. Write your time here. ⬭

The squirrel quickly and quietly drank the liquid.

Check
☑ Tick the best joins from q.

Checklist
☐ The letters are equally spaced.
☐ All the x-height letters are the same size.
☐ The letter q is correctly formed.

Name _____ Date _____

Trace and write the joins.

ty   ty   tr   tr   te   te   ur   ur   um   um   up   up

_____

Read, trace and write the words. Time yourself. Write your time here. ⌷

empty   empty   cup cup   athlete   athlete

_____   _____   _____

turn   turn   jumped   jumped   triumph   triumph

_____   _____   _____

Read, trace and write the sentence. Time yourself. Write your time here. ⌷

The triumphant athlete jumped up with the cup.

_____

_____

Check
☑ Tick the best joins from *t*.
☑ Tick the best joins from *u*.

Checklist
☐ The letters are equally spaced.
☐ All ascenders are the same height except for *t* which is slightly shorter.
☐ The letters *t* and *u* are correctly formed.

Name .... Date ....

Trace and write the joins.

tu   tu   tl   tl   am   am   cr   cr   ie   ie   ue   ue

Read, trace and write the words. Time yourself. Write your time here. ⬭

turtle turtle   swam swam   across across

friends friends   blue blue   ocean ocean

Read, trace and write the sentence. Time yourself. Write your time here. ⬭

The turtle and his friends swam across the blue

ocean.

Check
☑ Tick the words with the best spacing between the letters.

Checklist
☐ The letters are equally spaced.
☐ All the x-height letters are the same size.
☐ All the ascenders are the same height.
☐ All ascenders are the same height except for *t* which is slightly shorter.
☐ All the letters are correctly formed.

Name _____ Date _____

Trace and write the joins.

ad   ad   ag   ag   ac   ac   cc   cc   ca   ca   co   co

_____

Read, trace and write the words. Time yourself. Write your time here. ⬭

address address agree agree academy academy

_____   _____   _____

successful   comical   communicate

_____   _____   _____

Read, trace and write the sentence. Time yourself. Write your time here. ⬭

The academy agreed that the show was comical.

_____

_____

Check
☑ Tick the best joins from *a*.
☑ Tick the best joins from *c*.

Checklist
☐ The letters are equally spaced.
☐ All the x-height letters are the same size.
☐ The letters *a* and *c* are correctly formed.
☐ The joins from *a* and *c* are long enough for the next letter to start in the right place (1 o'clock).

Name .... Date ....

Trace and write the joins.

da   da   dg   dg   dd   dd   ec   ec   ea   ea   ed   ed

_____

Read, trace and write the words. Time yourself. Write your time here. ⬭

address address   badge badge   adder adder

_____   _____   _____

dangerous   secondary   learned

_____   _____   _____

Read, trace and write the sentence. Time yourself. Write your time here. ⬭

I won a badge because I learned that adders

mean danger.

_____

_____

Check
☑ Tick the best joins from *d*.
☑ Tick the best joins from *e*.

Checklist
☐ The letters are equally spaced.
☐ All the x-height letters are the same size.
☐ The letters *d* and *e* are correctly formed.
☐ The joins from *d* and *e* are long enough for the next letter to start in the right place (1 o'clock).

Unit 19: Diagonal join to an anticlockwise letter from *h* and *i*

Name .... Date ....

Trace and write the joins.

hd hd hc hc ho ho ia ia ig ig ic ic

_____

Read, trace and write the words. Time yourself. Write your time here. ☐

birthday birthday dishcloth dishcloth picnic picnic

_____ _____ _____

enthusiastic   gigantic   photographic

_____ _____ _____

Read, trace and write the sentence. Time yourself. Write your time here. ☐

Behold the photograph of my gigantic
birthday picnic!

_____

_____

Check
☑ Tick the best joins from *h*.
☑ Tick the best joins from *i*.

Checklist
☐ The letters are equally spaced.
☐ All the x-height letters are the same size.
☐ The letters *h* and *i* are correctly formed.
☐ The joins from *h* and *i* are long enough for the next letter to start in the right place (1 o'clock).

Name .... Date ....

Trace and write the joins.

ko ko ka ka ks ks la la lg lg ld ld

_____

Read, trace and write the words. Time yourself. Write your time here. ⬭

lookout lookout   koala koala   books books

_____   _____   _____

kangaroo kangaroo bulge bulge golden golden

_____   _____   _____

Read, trace and write the sentence. Time yourself. Write your time here. ⬭

We kept a lookout for books about koalas and

kangaroos.

_____

_____

Check
☑ Tick the best joins from _k_.
☑ Tick the best joins from _l_.

Checklist
☐ The letters are equally spaced.
☐ The ascenders are the same height and parallel.
☐ The letters _k_ and _l_ are correctly formed.
☐ The joins from _k_ and _l_ are long enough for the next
    letter to start in the right place (1 o'clock).

Name .... Date ....

Trace and write the joins.

mo mo ma ma mc mc nc nc nd nd ng ng

_____

Read, trace and write the words. Time yourself. Write your time here. ⬭

end end   damage damage   armchair armchair

_____   _____   _____

performance   morning   dancing

_____   _____   _____

Read, trace and write the sentence. Time yourself. Write your time here. ⬭

The dancing at the end of the performance

damaged the floor.

_____

_____

Check
☑ Tick the best joins from *m*.
☑ Tick the best joins from *n*.

Checklist
☐ The letters are equally spaced.
☐ All the x-height letters are the same size.
☐ The joins from *m* and *n* are correctly formed.
☐ The joins from *m* and *n* are long enough for the next letter to start in the right place (1 o'clock).

Name .... Date ....

Trace and write the joins.

tc   tc   td   td   ta   ta   ua   ua   uc   uc   ug   ug

Read, trace and write the words. Time yourself. Write your time here. ⬭

catch catch   hotdog hotdog   taught taught

equal equal   touch touch   enough enough

Read, trace and write the sentence. Time yourself. Write your time here. ⬭

In rugby, I was gradually taught to catch and

make touch-downs.

Check
☑ Tick the best joins from *t*.
☑ Tick the best joins from *u*.

Checklist
☐ The letters are equally spaced.
☐ All the x-height letters are the same size, and *t* is slightly taller.
☐ The joins from *t* and *u* are long enough for the next letter to start in the right place (1 o'clock).

Name .... Date ....

Trace and write the joins.

alt tho hal mam mal lph ins eat the air

_____

Read, trace and write the words. Time yourself. Write your time here. ⬭

although although air air mammal mammal

_____ _____ _____

dolphins dolphins breathe breathe whale whale

_____ _____ _____

Read, trace and write the sentence. Time yourself. Write your time here. ⬭

Whales and dolphins are mammals. They
breathe air.

_____

_____

Check
☑ Tick the words with the best joins.
☑ Tick the words with the best spacing between letters.

Checklist
☐ The letters are equally spaced.
☐ All the x-height letters are the same size.
☐ All the ascenders are the same height.
☐ All the letters are correctly formed.
☐ All joins to anticlockwise letters start at 1 o'clock.

Name .... Date ....

Trace and write the joins.

tig tig   oar oar   ung ung   ian ian   nke nke

Read, trace and write the words. Time yourself. Write your time here. ⬭

tiger tiger   roared roared   jungle jungle

Indian Indian   deep deep   monkey monkey

Read, trace and write the sentence. Time yourself. Write your time here. ⬭

Deep in an Indian jungle, the tiger roared at the monkey.

Check
☑ Tick the words with the best joins.
☑ Tick the words with the best spacing between letters.

Checklist
☐ The letters are equally spaced.
☐ All the x-height letters are the same size.
☐ All the ascenders are the same height.
☐ All the joins are correctly formed.
☐ All joins to anticlockwise letters start at 1 o'clock.

Name .... Date ....

Trace and write the joins.

oh oh ot ot ol ol wb wb wl wl wh wh

_____

Read, trace and write the words. Time yourself. Write your time here. ( )

John John   got got   snowballs snowballs

_____   _____   _____

told told   scowled scowled   when when

_____   _____   _____

Read, trace and write the sentence. Time yourself. Write your time here. ( )

John scowled when he got told not to throw

snowballs.

_____

_____

Check
☑ Tick the best joins from *o*.
☑ Tick the best joins from *w*.

Checklist
☐ The letters are equally spaced.
☐ All the x-height letters are the same size.
☐ The letters *o* and *w* are correctly formed.
☐ The joins from *o* and *w* are long enough for the next letter to start in the right place at the top of the ascender.

Name .... Date ....

Trace and write the joins.

oi   oi   ow   ow   on   on   or   or   op   op   oe   oe

Read, trace and write the words. Time yourself. Write your time here. ⬭

poison poison   order order   work work

tomorrow   opportunity   volcanoes

Read, trace and write the sentence. Time yourself. Write your time here. ⬭

Tomorrow, he has the opportunity to work on

volcanoes.

Check
☑ Tick the best joins from *o*.

Checklist
☐ The letters are equally spaced.
☐ All the x-height letters are the same height.
☐ The letter *o* is correctly formed and closed at the top.
☐ The join from *o* is long enough for the next letter to
   start in the right place (1 o'clock).

Name .... Date ....

Trace and write the joins.

ve   ve   vi   vi   vy   vy   wr   wr   wu   wu   we   we

_____

Read, trace and write the words. Time yourself. Write your time here. ⌇⌇⌇⌇⌇⌇

have   have   review   review   heavy   heavy

_____   _____   _____

writing   writing   swung   swung   vowels   vowels

_____   _____   _____

Read, trace and write the sentence. Time yourself. Write your time here. ⌇⌇⌇⌇⌇⌇

I'm reviewing the vowels in my handwriting.

I'm doing very well!

_____

_____

Check
☑ Tick the best joins from *v*.
☑ Tick the best joins from *w*.

Checklist
☐ The letters are equally spaced.
☐ All the x-height letters are the same height.
☐ The letters *v* and *w* are correctly formed.
☐ The joins from *v* and *w* are long enough for the next letter to start in the right place (1 o'clock).

Name .... Date ....

Trace and write the joins.

oo oo oa oa oc oc od od og og oq oq

_____

Read, trace and write the words. Time yourself. Write your time here. ⬭

looked looked   throat throat   doctor doctor

_____   _____   _____

today today   frog frog   croquet croquet

_____   _____   _____

Read, trace and write the sentence. Time yourself. Write your time here. ⬭

Today, the doctor looked for the frog in my

throat.

_____

_____

Check
☑ Tick the best joins from o.

Checklist
☐ The letters are equally spaced.
☐ All the x-height letters are the same height.
☐ The letter o is correctly formed and closed at the top.
☐ The join from o is long enough for the next letter to start in the right place (1 o'clock).

Name .... Date ....

Trace and write the joins.

va va vo vo wa wa wo wo wc wc wd wd

Read, trace and write the words. Time yourself. Write your time here. ⬭

festival festival   avoided avoided   was was

two two   newcomer newcomer   crowd crowd

Read, trace and write the sentence. Time yourself. Write your time here. ⬭

The two newcomers avoided the festival crowd.

Check
☑ Tick the best joins from *v*.
☑ Tick the best joins from *w*.

Checklist
☐ The letters are equally spaced.
☐ All the x-height letters are the same height.
☐ The letters *v* and *w* are correctly formed.
☐ The joins from *v* and *w* are long enough for the next letter to start in the right place (1 o'clock).

Name .... Date ....

Trace and write the joins.

won won woo woo ool ool wh wh ove ove ow ow

Read, trace and write the words. Time yourself. Write your time here.

wonder wonder   woollen woollen   whole whole

glove glove   bowl bowl   throat throat

Read, trace and write the sentence. Time yourself. Write your time here.

Steve wondered why people wore warm

woollen gloves.

Check
☑ Tick the words with the best horizontal joins.

Checklist
☐ The horizontal joins are long enough for the next letter to start in the right place (1 o'clock).
☐ The letters are equally spaced.
☐ All the x-height letters are the same height.
☐ All the ascenders are parallel.

Name .... Date ....

Trace and write the joins.

sp   sp   sh   sh   st   st   sm   sm   su   su   sw   sw

_____

Read, trace and write the words. Time yourself. Write your time here. ⬭

spoil spoil   *she she*   *dentist dentist*

_____   _____   _____

smile smile   *suffer suffer*   *sweets sweets*

_____   _____   _____

Read, trace and write the sentence. Time yourself. Write your time here. ⬭

The dentist said that too many sweets can

spoil your smile.

_____

_____

Check
☑ Tick the words with the best joins from *s*.

Checklist
☐ The *s* is formed correctly before the join begins.
☐ All the x-height letters are the same height.
☐ The letters are equally spaced.

Name .... Date ....

Trace and write the joins.

ss   ss   sa   sa   sc   sc   so   so   sd   sd   sg   sg

Read, trace and write the words. Time yourself. Write your time here. ⬭

lesson lesson   safety safety   science science

discussed   Wednesday   disguise

Read, trace and write the sentence. Time yourself. Write your time here. ⬭

In our science lesson on Wednesday we
discussed safety.

Check
☑ Tick the words with the best joins from s.

Checklist
☐ The s is formed correctly before the join begins.
☐ The join from s is long enough for the next letter to start in the right place (1 o'clock).
☐ All the x-height letters are the same height.
☐ The letters are equally spaced.

Unit 33: Joining from *b*

Name .... Date ....

Trace and write the joins.

bbl bbl br br be be by by bs bs ba ba

Read, trace and write the words. Time yourself. Write your time here. ☐

brave brave   babble babble   bellow bellow

baby baby   climbs climbs   beanbag beanbag

Read, trace and write the sentence. Time yourself. Write your time here. ☐

The brave baby climbs onto the beanbag and

babbles.

Check
☑ Tick the words with the best joins from *b*.

Checklist
☐ The letter *b* is fully closed before the join begins.
☐ The letters are equally spaced.
☐ All the x-height letters are the same height.
☐ All the ascenders are parallel and the same height.

Name .... Date ....

Trace and write the joins.

pl   pl   pe   pe   pr   pr   po   po   pp   pp   ps   ps

Read, trace and write the words. Time yourself. Write your time here. ⬭

planet   planet   people   people   protect   protect

pollution pollution   appeal appeal   perhaps perhaps

Read, trace and write the sentence. Time yourself. Write your time here. ⬭

All people should protect the planet from

pollution.

Check
☑ Tick the words with the best joins from *p*.

Checklist
☐ The letter *p* is fully closed before the join begins.
☐ The letters are equally spaced.
☐ All the descenders are parallel and the same height.

Name .... Date ....

Trace and write the joins.

_af af ef ef kf kf sf sf of of wf wf_

_____

Read, trace and write the words. Time yourself. Write your time here. ⬭

after after before before breakfast breakfast

_____   _____   _____

satisfied satisfied   often often   awful awful

_____   _____   _____

Read, trace and write the sentence. Time yourself. Write your time here. ⬭

Before breakfast I am often hungry, but

afterwards I am satisfied.

_____

_____

Check
☑ Tick the words with the best joins from _f._

Checklist
☐ When joining to _f_ the letter starts by retracing the curve.
☐ The letters are equally spaced.
☐ All the ascenders and descenders are parallel.

Name _____ Date _____

Trace and write the joins.

afe afe nfe nfe sfo sfo iffi iffi lft lft offi offi

_____

Read, trace and write the words. Time yourself. Write your time here. ⬭

safe safe   *infect infect*   *transform transform*

_____   _____   _____

twelfth twelfth *difficult difficult* *official official*

_____   _____   _____

Read, trace and write the sentence. Time yourself. Write your time here. ⬭

It's difficult to spell official, confidence,

infectious and twelfth.

_____

_____

Check
- ☑ Tick the words with the best joins to *f*.
- ☑ Tick the words with the best joins from *f*.

Checklist
- ☐ When joining to *f* the letter starts by retracing the curve.
- ☐ The joins to and from *f* are accurate.
- ☐ The letters are equally spaced.
- ☐ All the ascenders and descenders are parallel.

Name .... Date ....

Trace and write the joins.

rl   rl   rt   rt   ri   ri   rp   rp   rr   rr   re   re

Read, trace and write the words. Time yourself. Write your time here.

arrive   arrive   surprise   surprise   nearly   nearly

ready   ready   return   return   birthday   birthday

Read, trace and write the sentence. Time yourself. Write your time here.

Fern's birthday surprise was nearly ready for
her arrival.

Check
☑ Tick the words with the best joins from *r*.

Checklist
☐ The join from *r* begins with a dip.
☐ The letters are equally spaced.
☐ All the x-height letters are the same size.

Name .... Date ....

Trace and write the joins.

ra   ra   rc   rc   rd   rd   rg   rg   ro   ro   rs   rs

_____

Read, trace and write the words. Time yourself. Write your time here. ( )

rather   rather   exercises   exercises   hard   hard

_____   _____   _____

energy   energy   front   front   mirrors   mirrors

_____   _____   _____

Read, trace and write the sentence. Time yourself. Write your time here. ( )

We did rather hard, energetic exercises in front

of mirrors.

_____

_____

Check
☑ Tick the words with the best joins from *r*.

Checklist
☐ The join from *r* begins with a dip.
☐ The join from *r* is long enough for the next letter to start in the right place.
☐ The letters are equally spaced.
☐ All the x-height letters are the same size.

Name .... Date ....

Trace and write the joins.

br   br   rs   rs   ed   ed   pe   pe   rf   rf   sc   sc

_____

Read, trace and write the words. Time yourself. Write your time here. ⬭

wanted   wanted   disco   disco   perfect   perfect

_____   _____   _____

school   school   brothers   brothers   look   look

_____   _____   _____

Read, trace and write the sentence. Time yourself. Write your time here. ⬭

The brothers all wanted to look perfect for the

school disco.

_____

_____

Check
☑ Tick the words with the best joins.

Checklist
☐ All the joins are written correctly.
☐ The letters are equally spaced.
☐ All the x-height letters are the same size.
☐ All the ascenders and descenders are parallel and the same height.

Name .... Date ....

Trace and write the joins.

ft ft re re fe fe ss ss sc sc sf sf

_____

Read, trace and write the words. Time yourself. Write your time here. ⬭

often often   preferred preferred   lessons lessons

_____   _____   _____

science science   successful successful   sisters sisters

_____   _____   _____

Read, trace and write the sentence. Time yourself. Write your time here. ⬭

The successful sisters often preferred science

lessons.

_____

_____

Check
☑ Tick the words with the best joins.

Checklist
☐ All the joins are written correctly.
☐ The letters are equally spaced.
☐ All the x-height letters are the same size.
☐ All the ascenders and descenders are parallel and the same height.

a b c d e f g h i j k l m n o p q r s t u v w x y z

Penpals
writing mat
for right-handers

A B C D E F G H I J K L M N O P Q R S T U V W X Y Z

a b c d e f g h i j k l m n o p q r s t u v w x y z

Penpals
writing mat
for left-handers

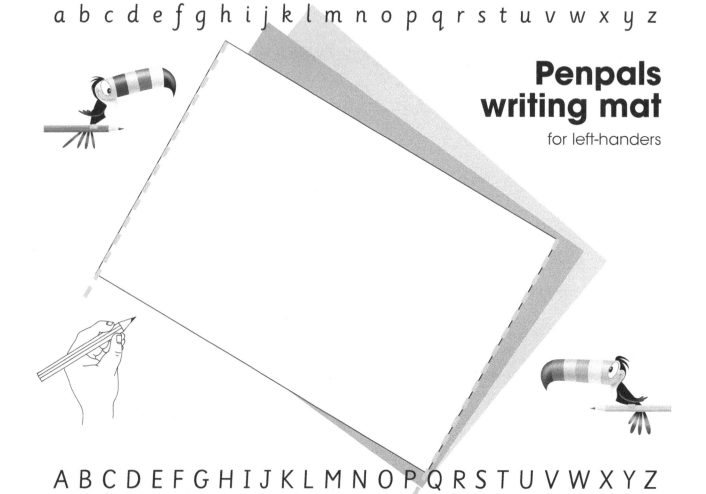

A B C D E F G H I J K L M N O P Q R S T U V W X Y Z